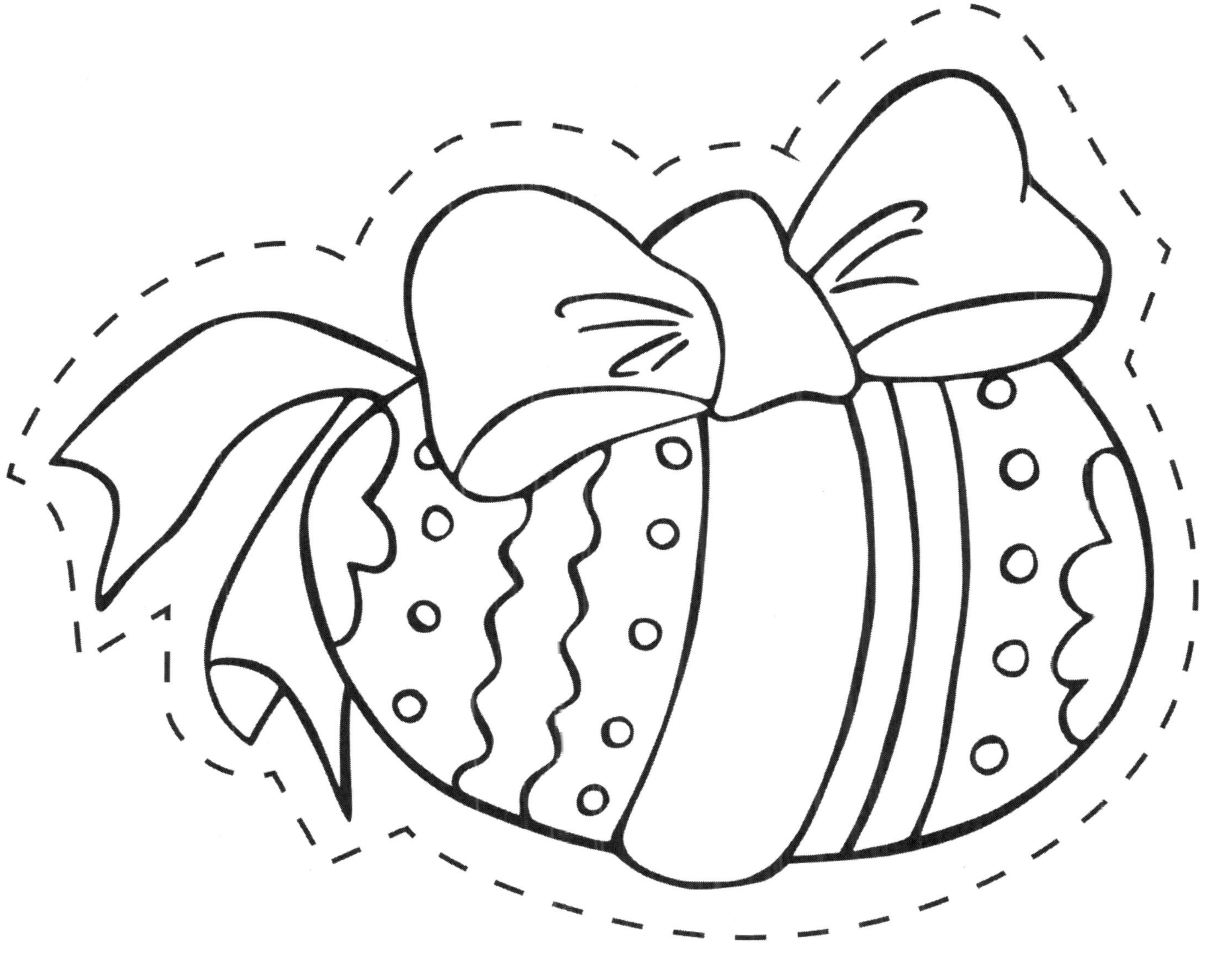

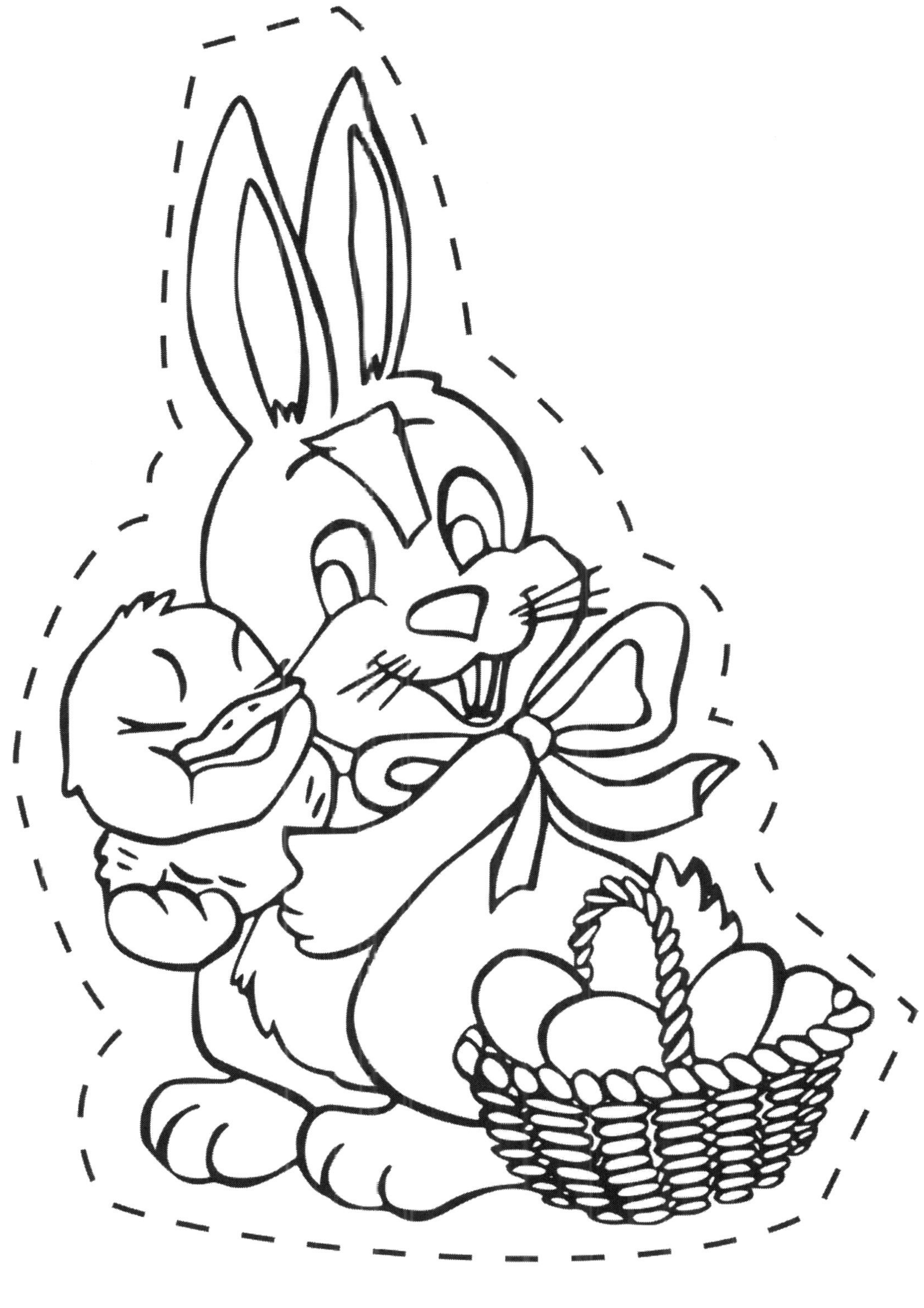

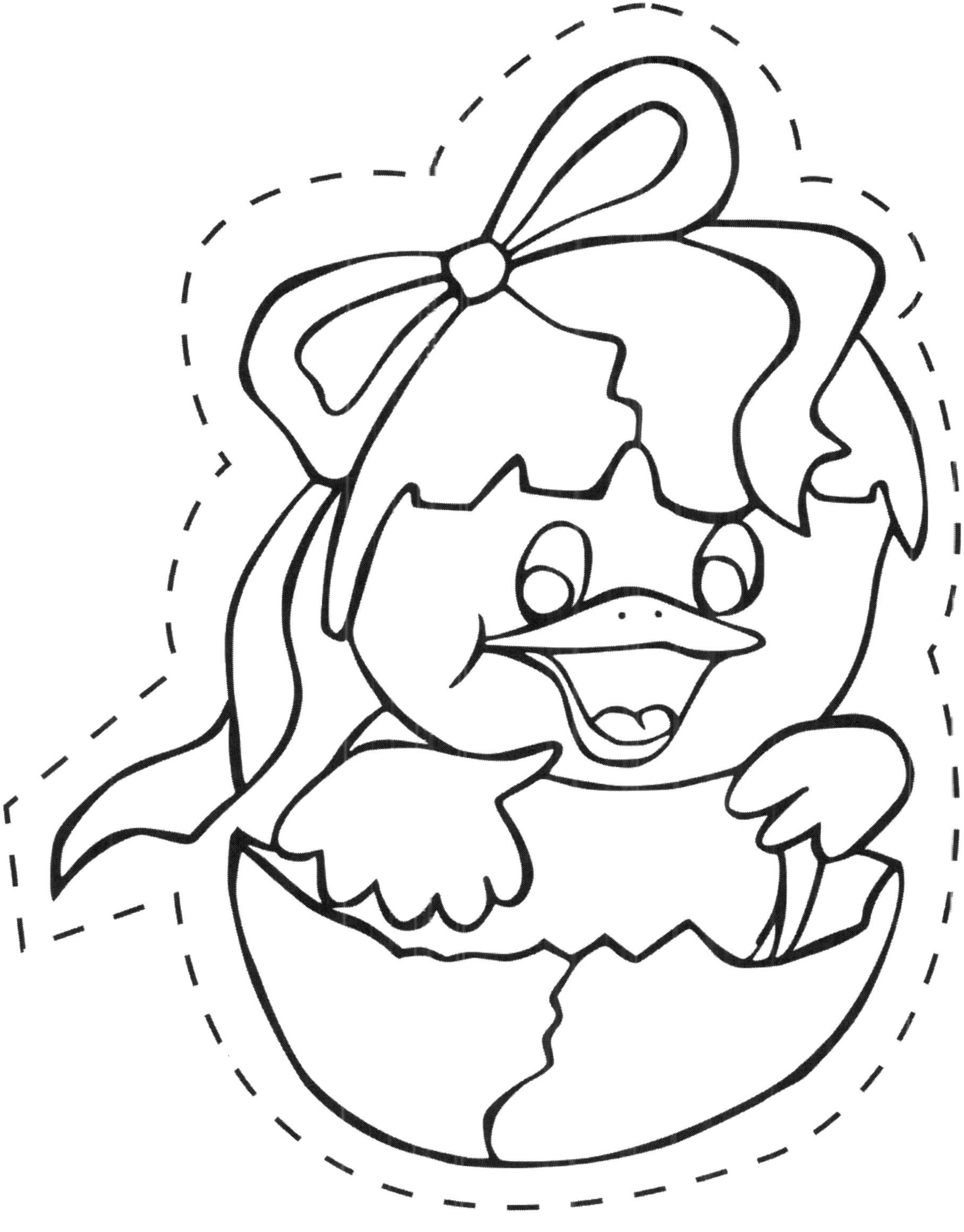

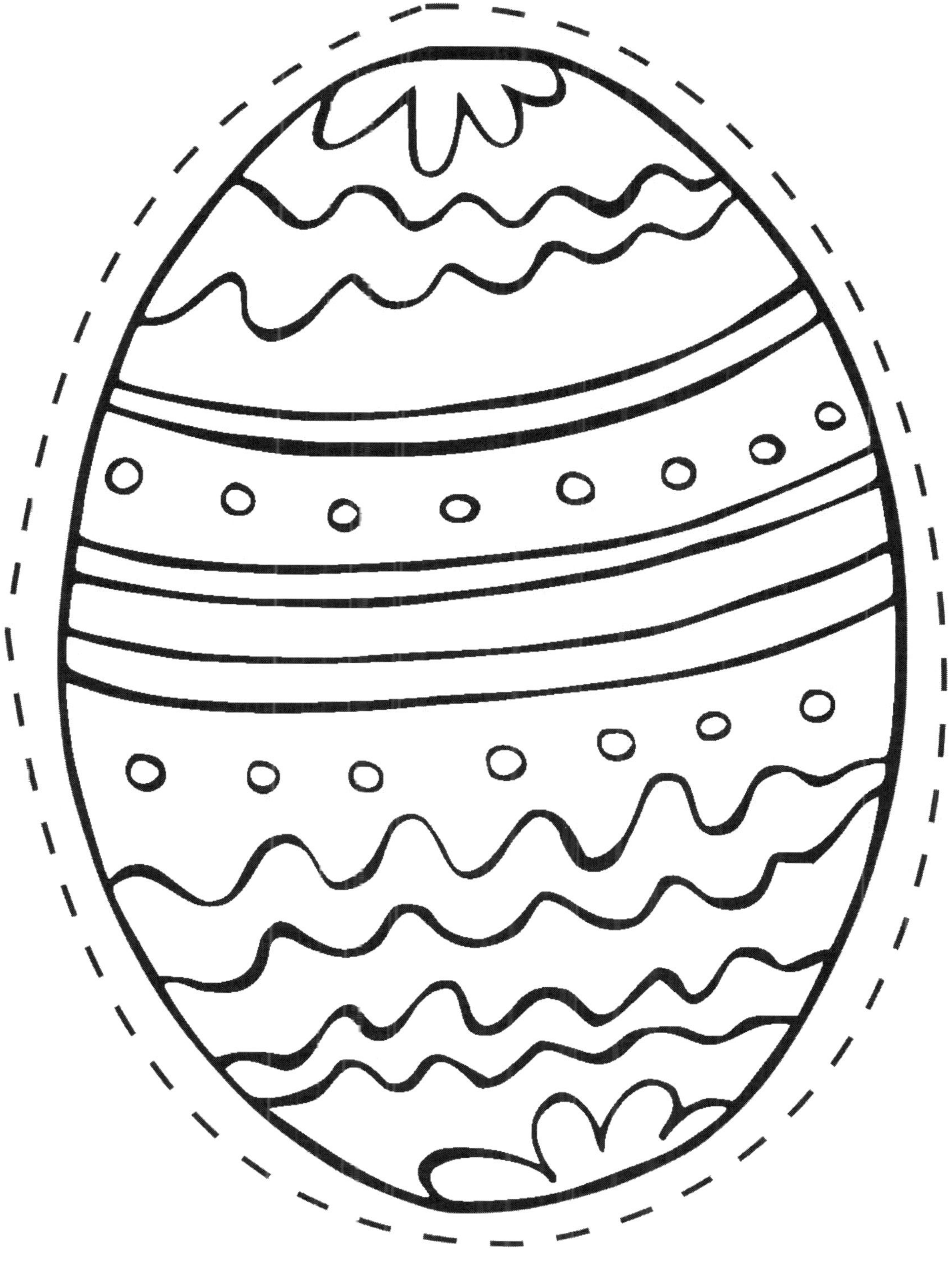

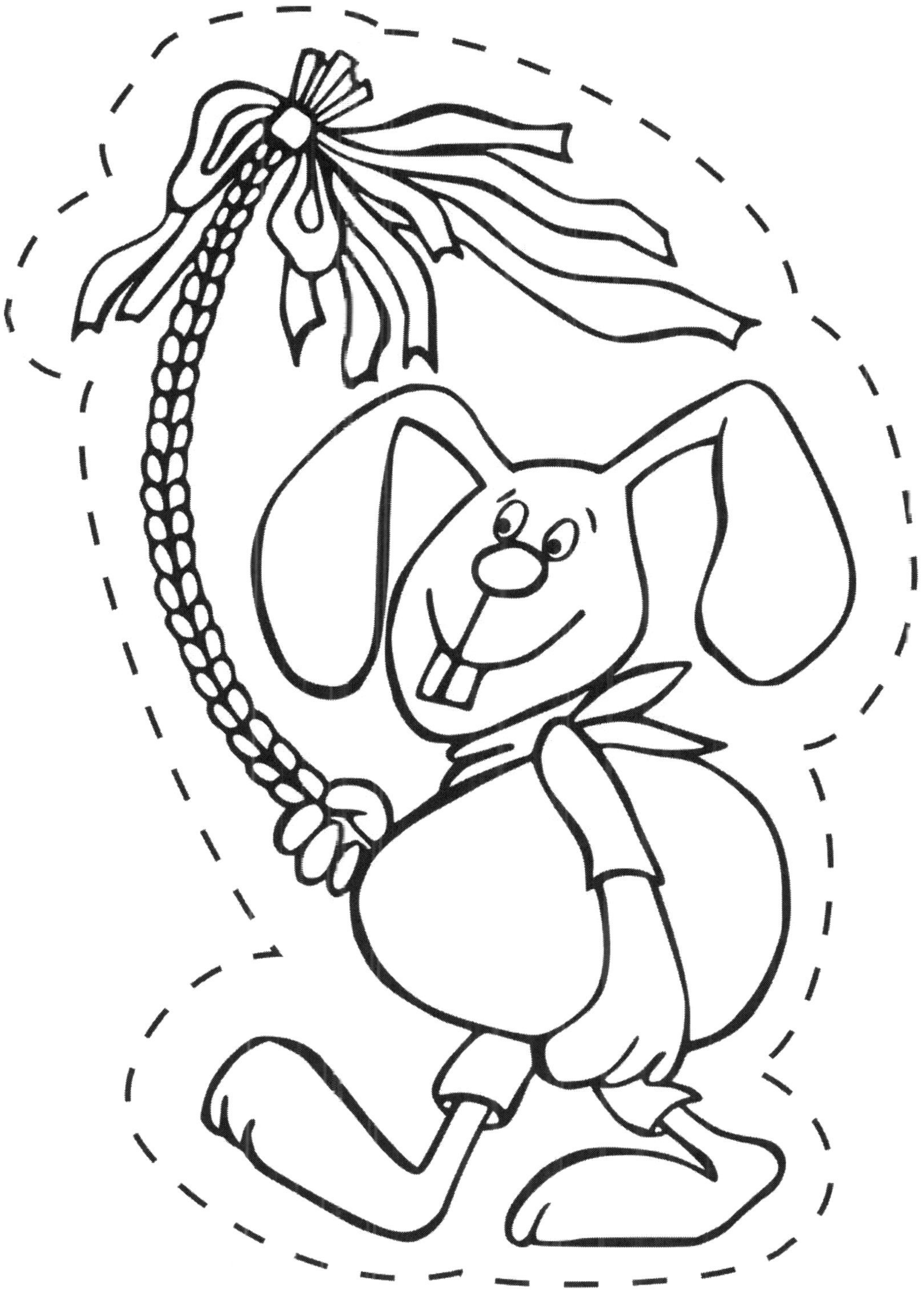

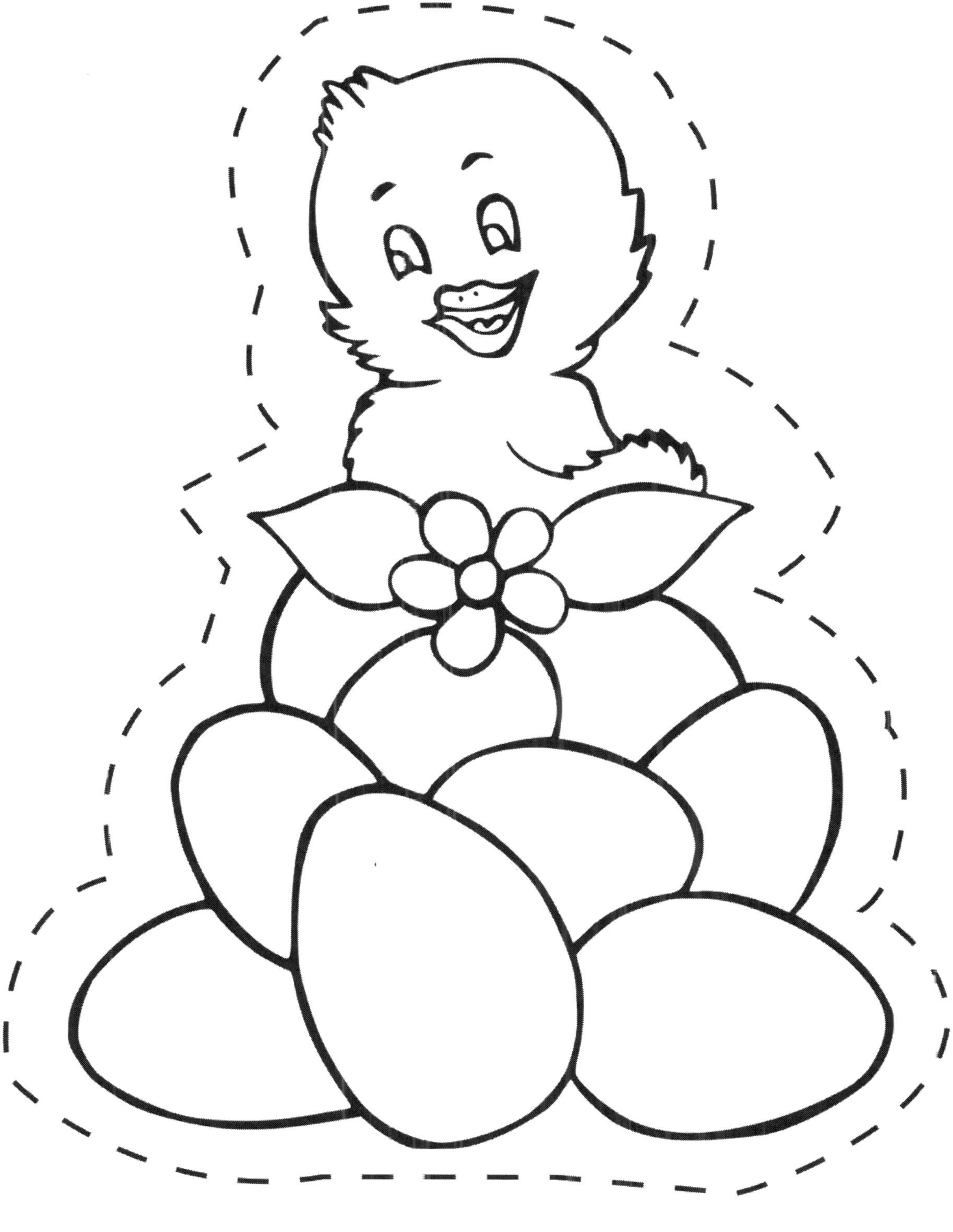

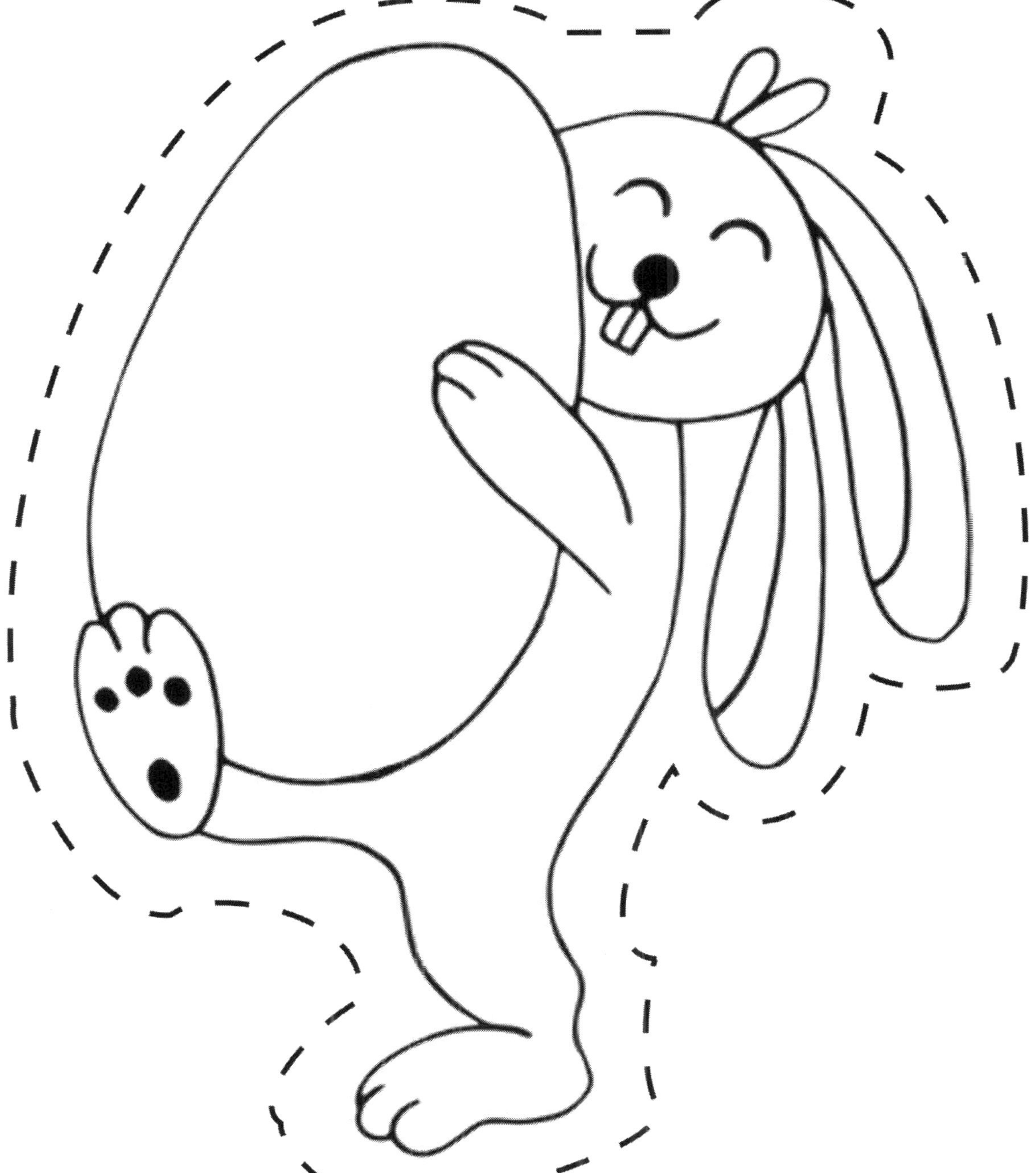

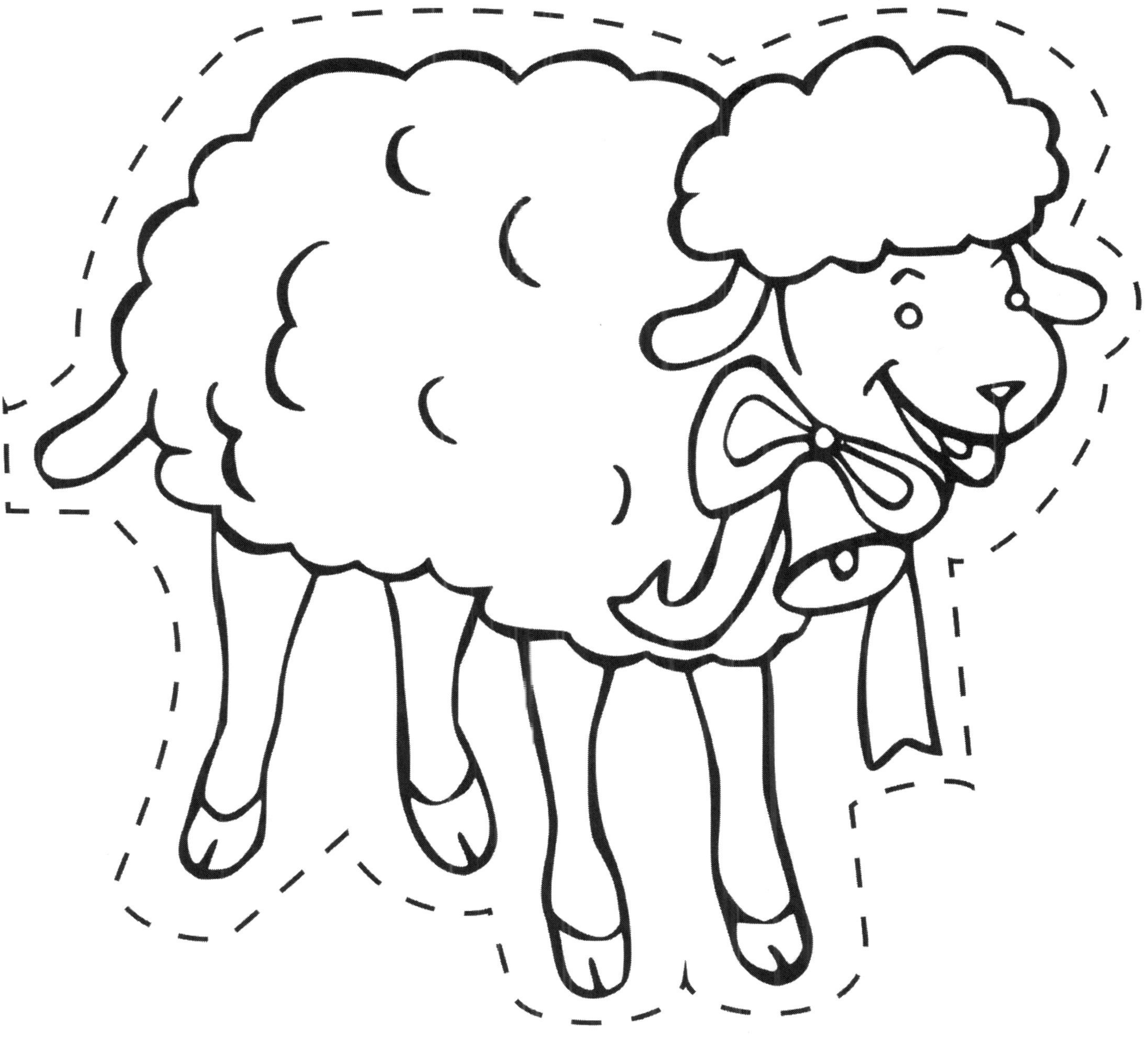

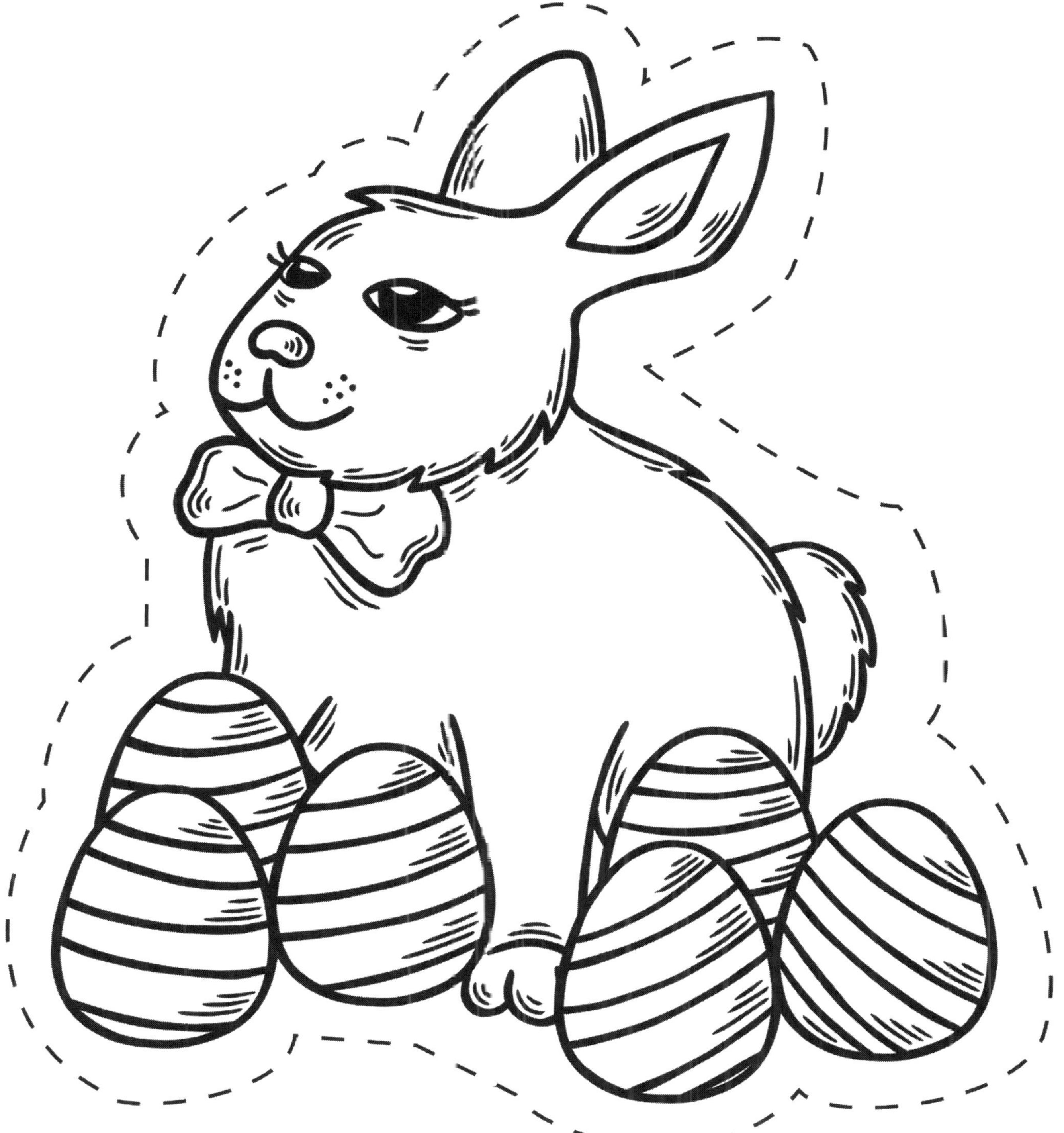

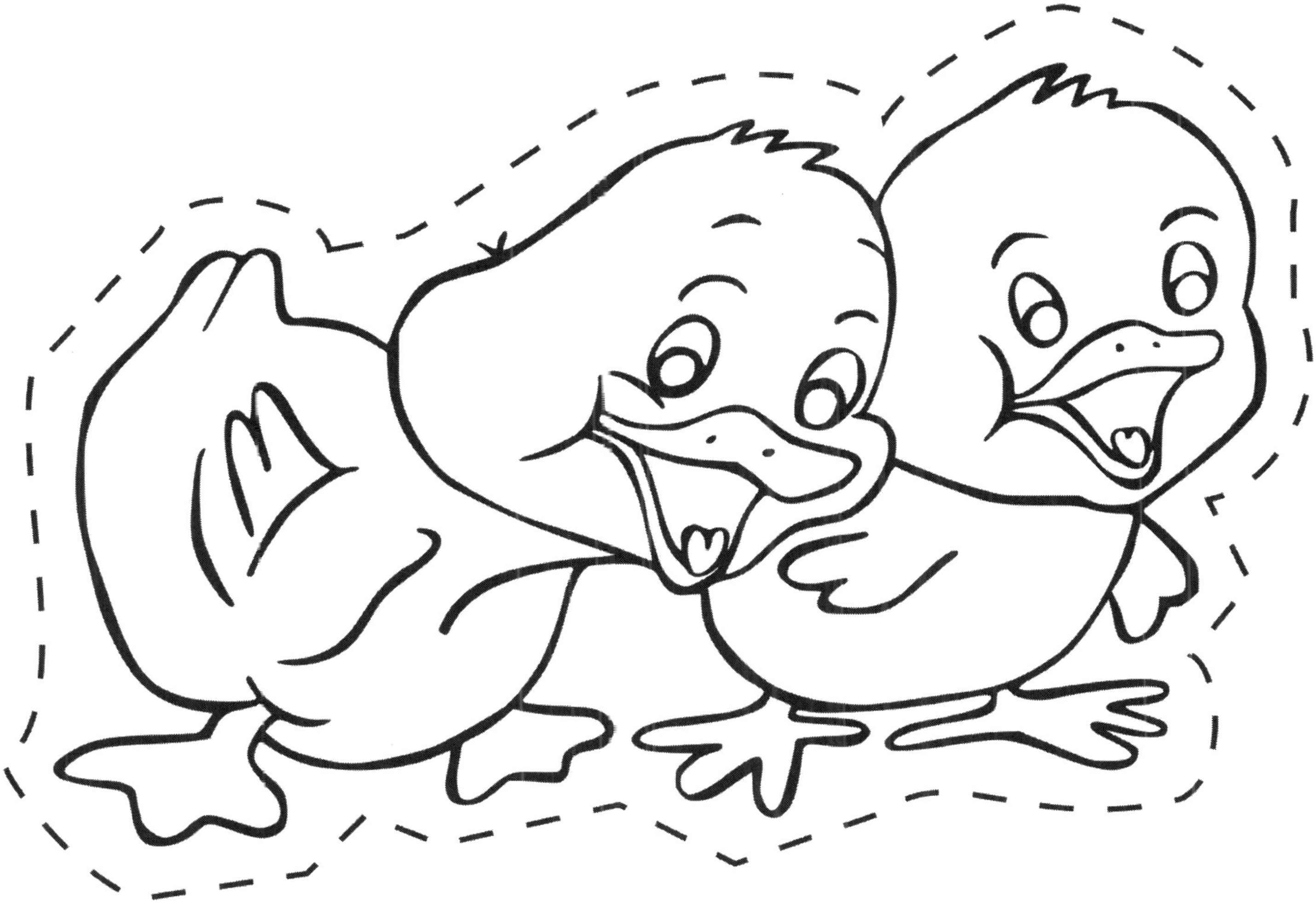

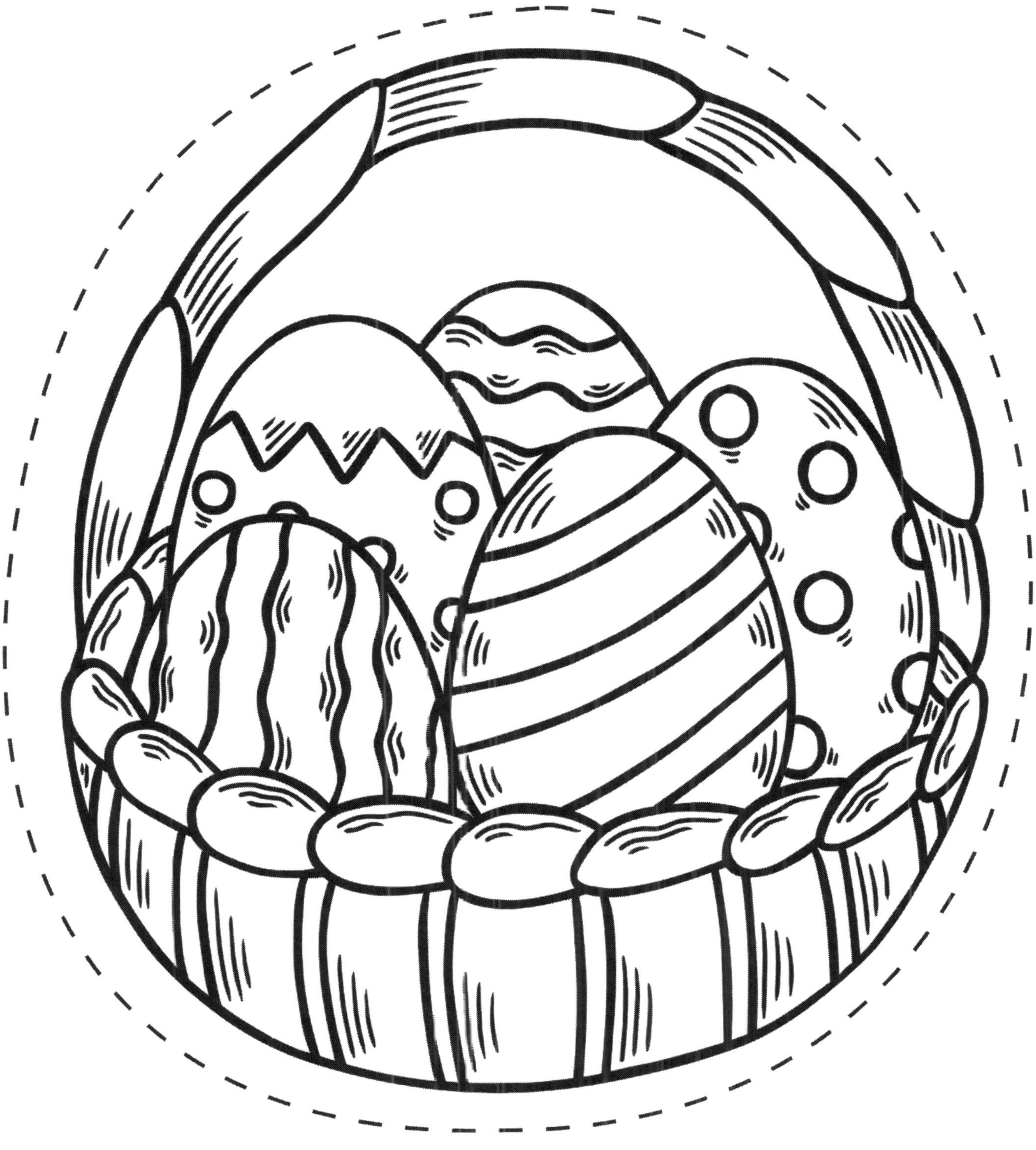

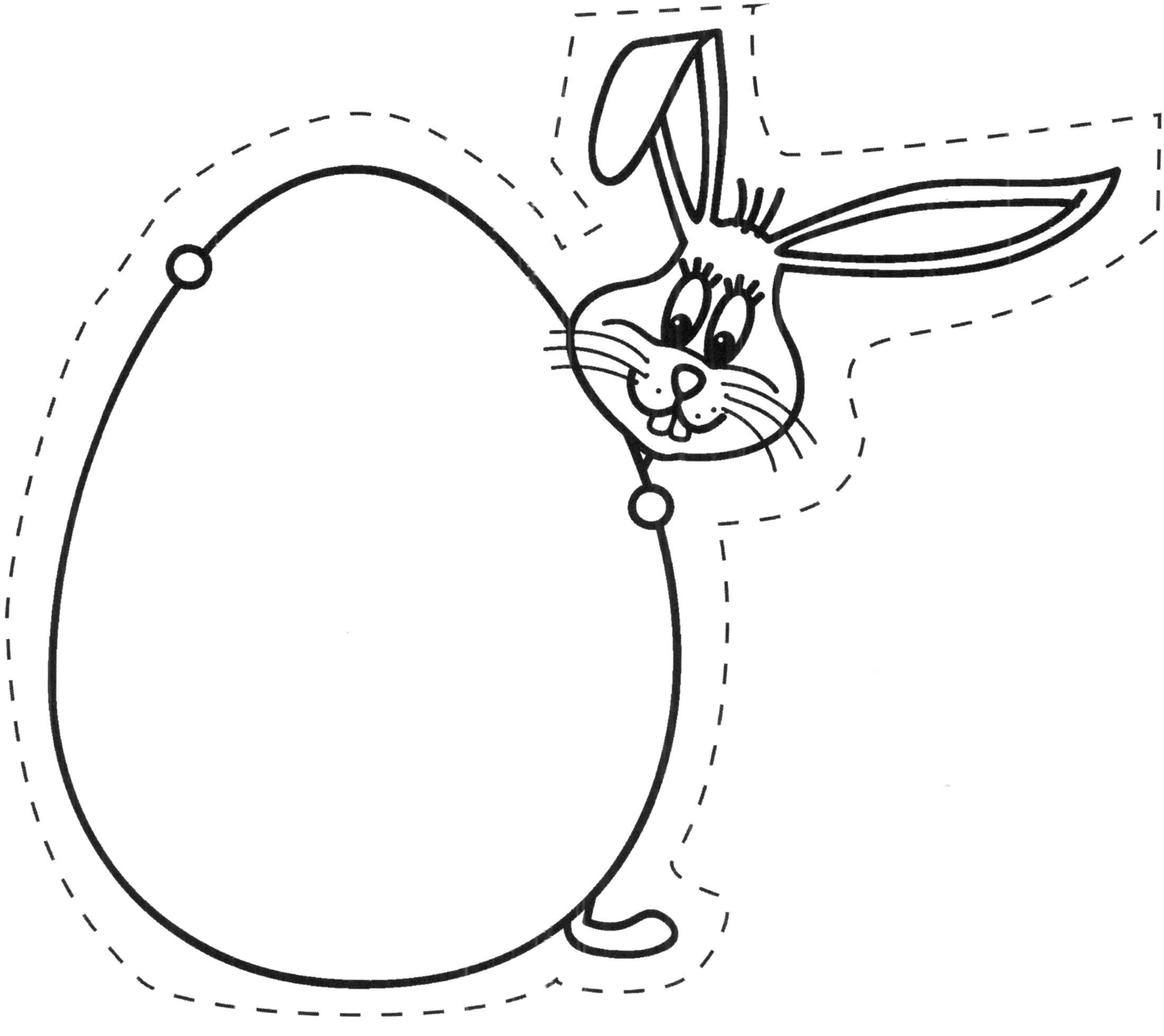

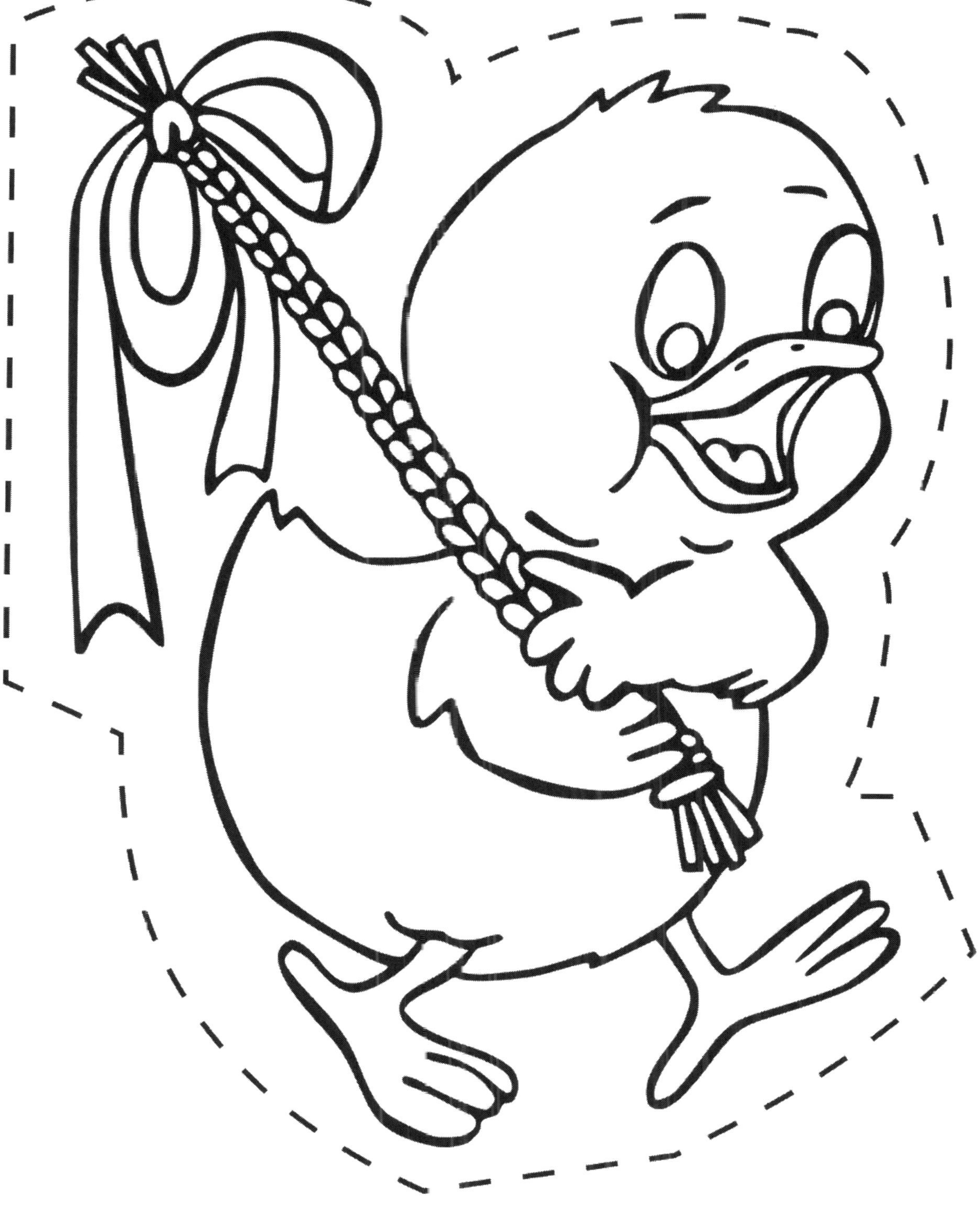

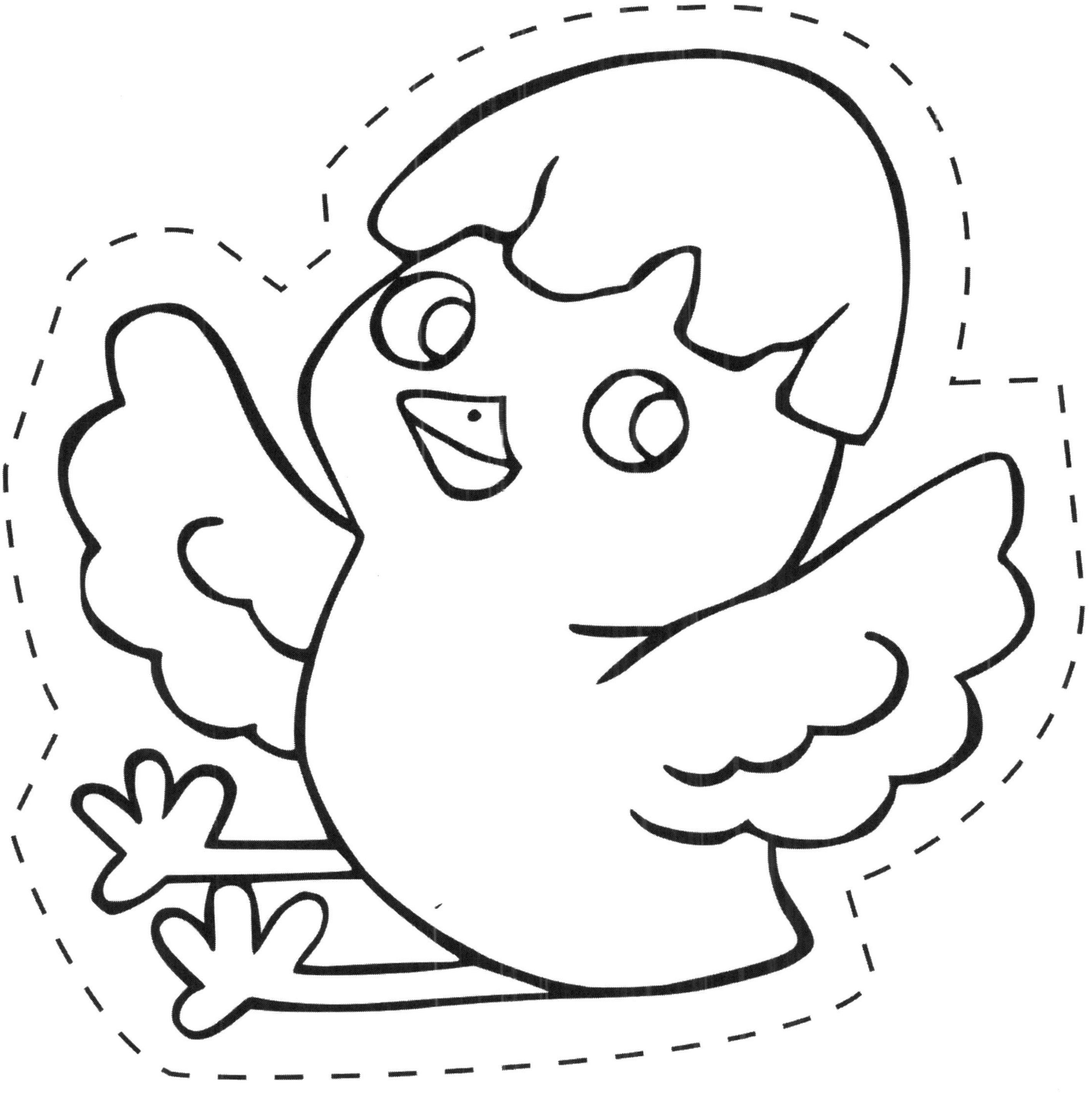

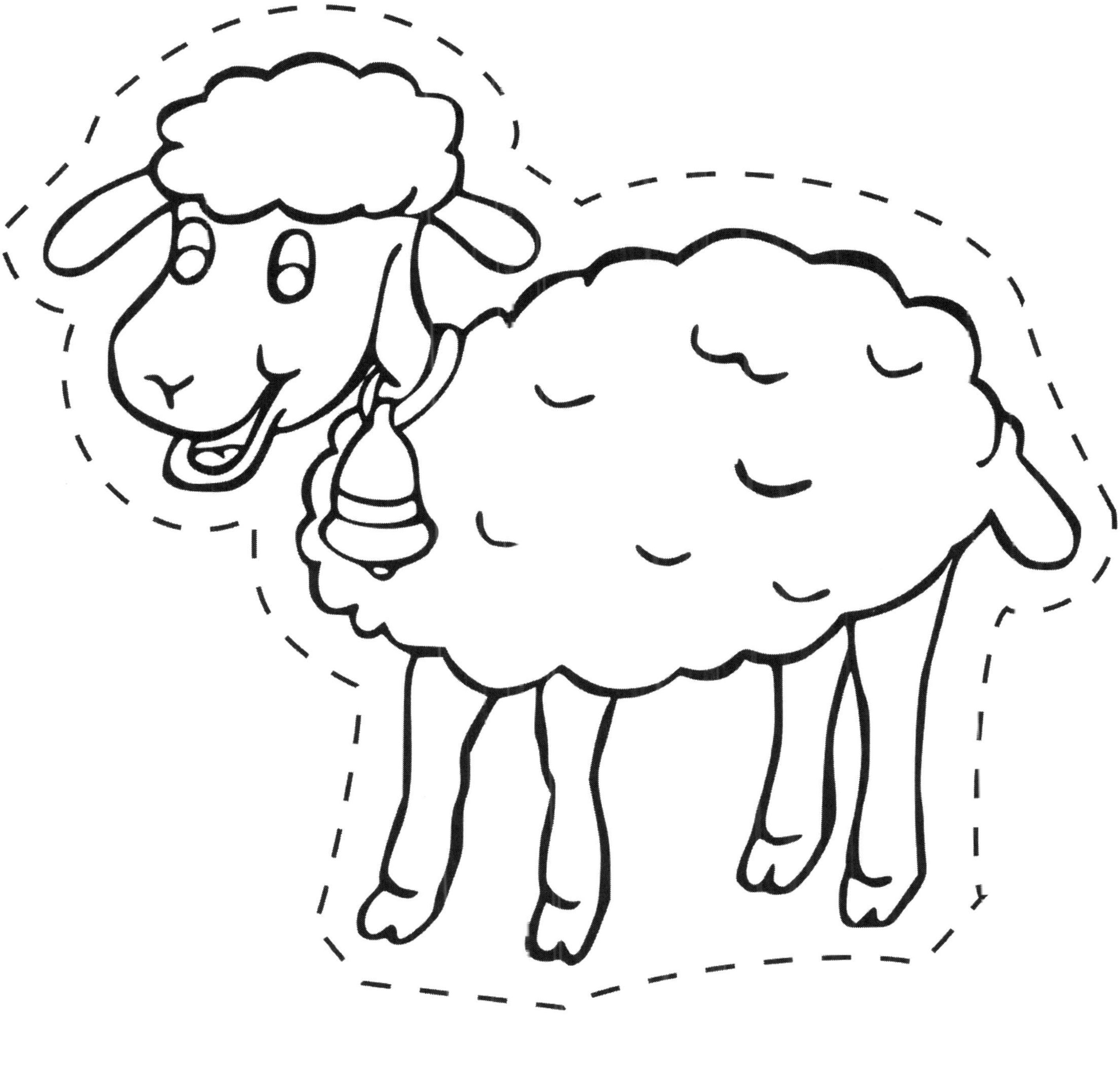

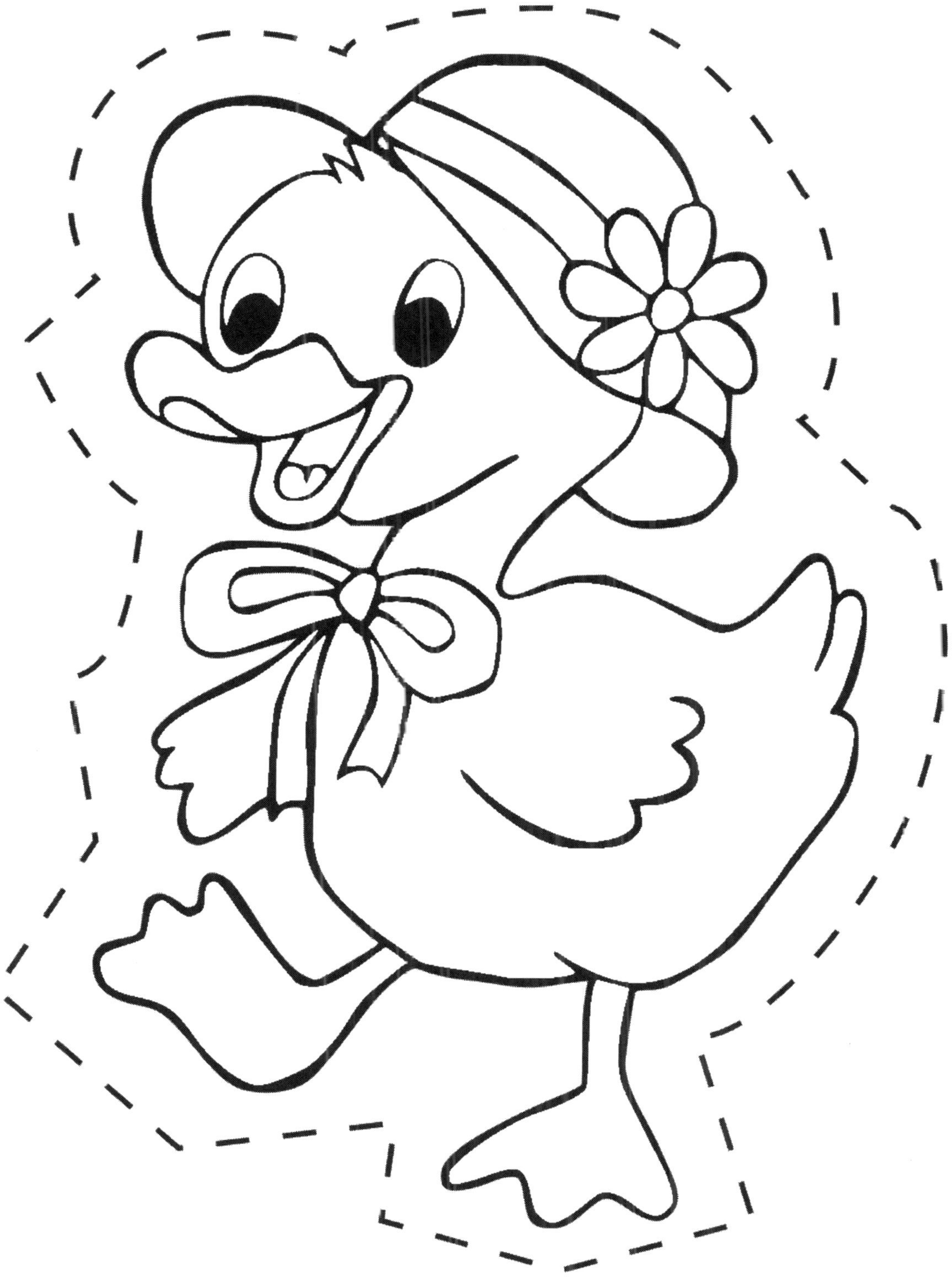

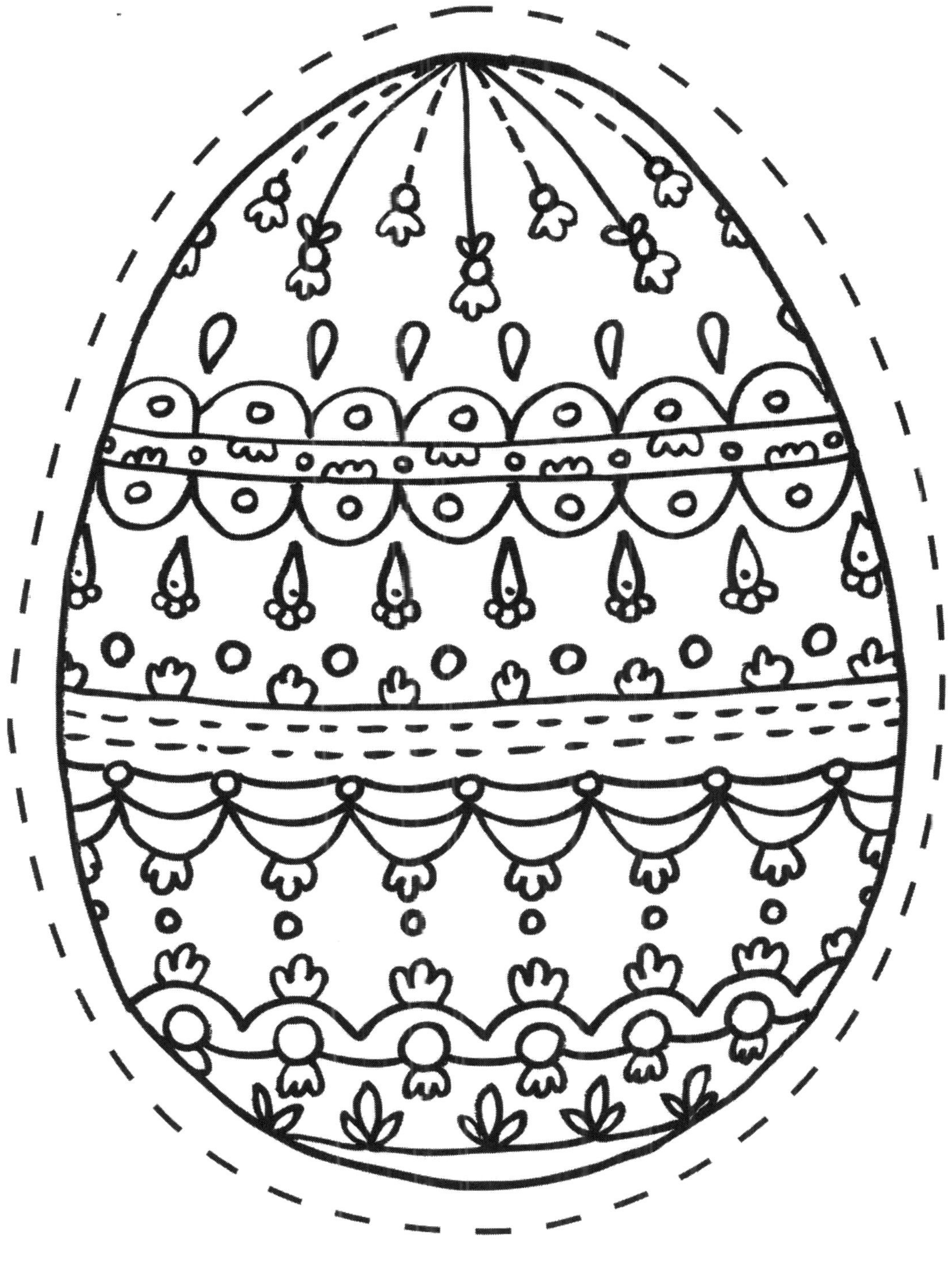

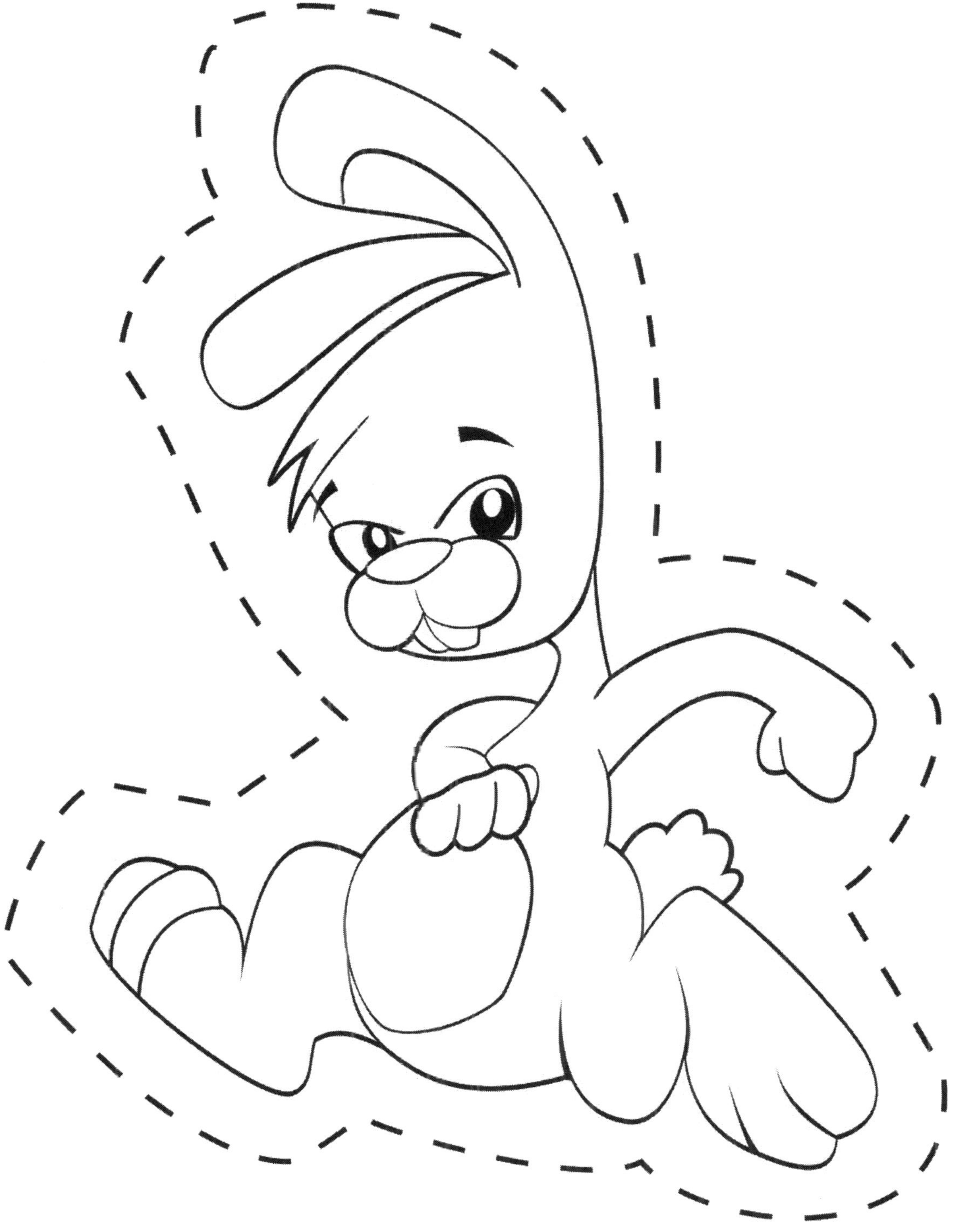

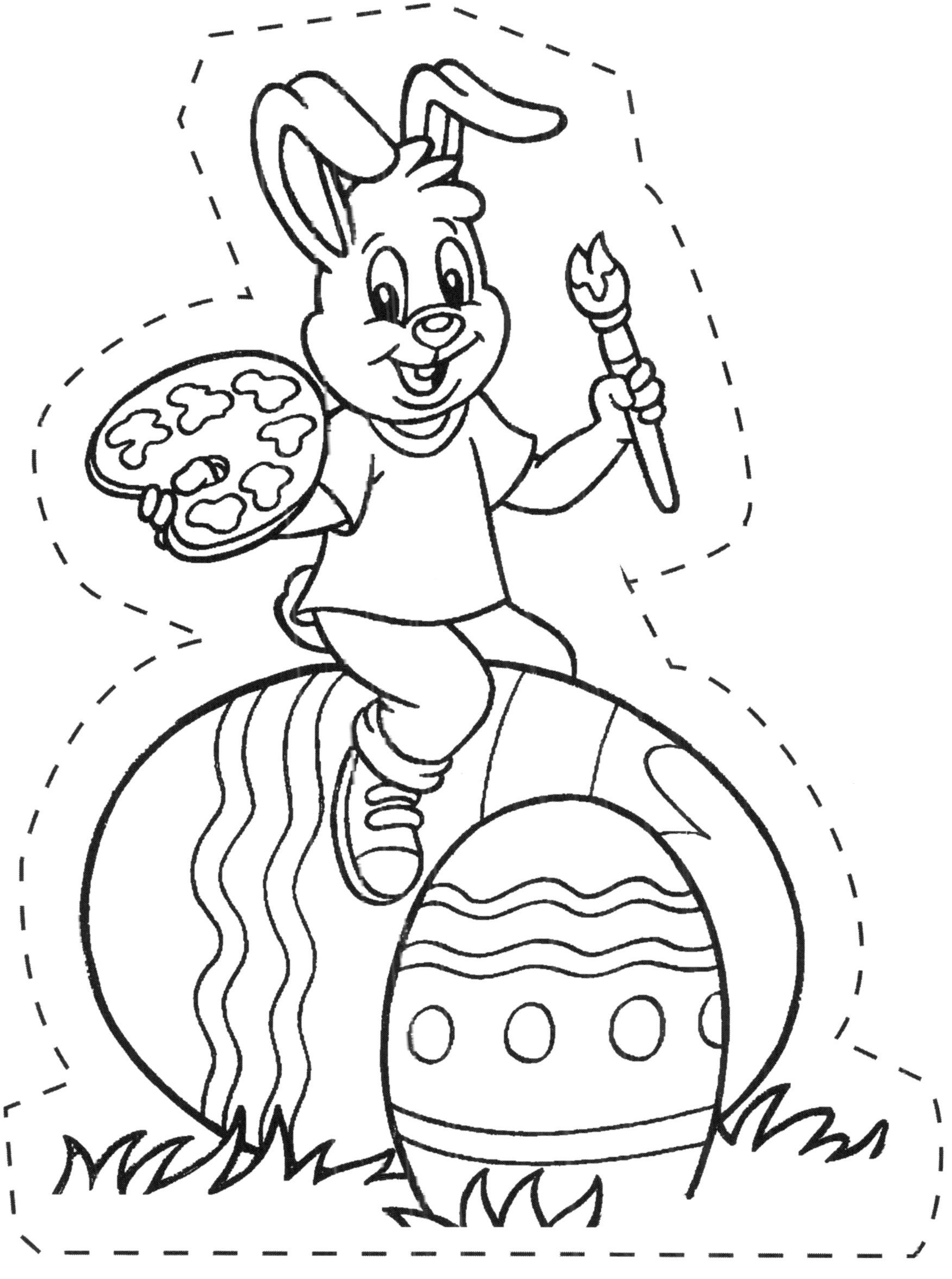

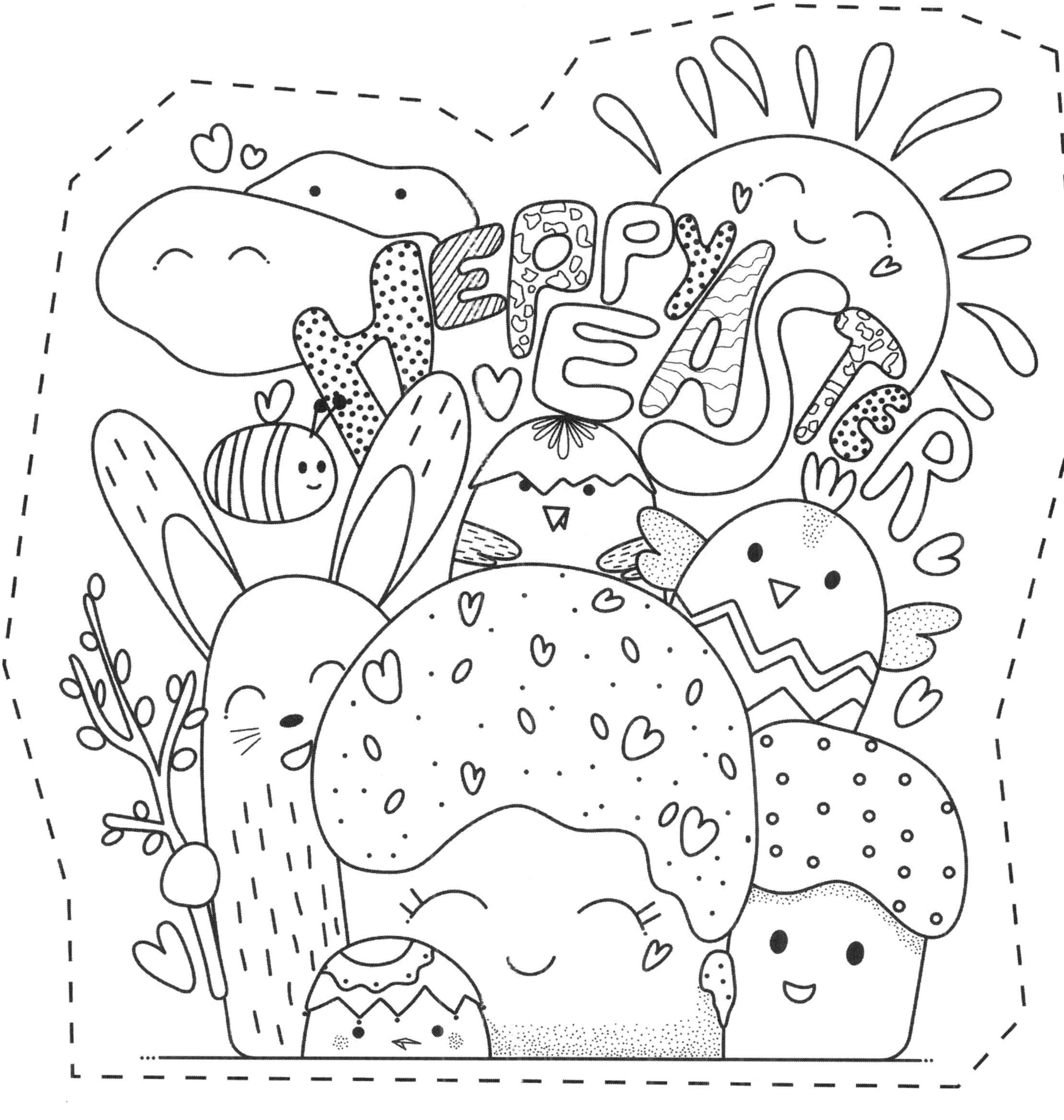
HAPPY EASTER

Made in the USA
Coppell, TX
27 March 2022

75633638R00022